I *ls ne sont pas Charlie!*
That is what should have been printed
on the T-shirts, scrawled across the placards,
and strung beside the trendy hashtags that
festooned cyberspace. It would have been a
slogan more befitting the throng that
descended on the City of Lights, particularly
the Western politicos – minus U.S. President
Barack Obama, the putative Leader From
Behind of the Formerly Free World.

Whatever these characters might be, they
most certainly are not Charlie.

It was nonetheless amid streaming "*Je Suis
Charlie*" banners that 40 high-government
officials led a crowd of more than 1.5 million
citizens in a "unity rally" at Place de la Répub-
lique. Millions more partook in concurrent
rallies throughout France. The ubiquitous signs
were in homage to *Charlie Hebdo*, a left-wing
satirical magazine featuring pungent cartoons
that proclaim a doctrinaire secularism. Earlier that week, editor in chief Stéphane Charbonnier, along with several *Charlie Hebdo*

cartoonists and columnists, had been brutally murdered at the start of a three-day jihadist rampage. When the smoke cleared, 17 innocents had been mowed down by gunfire in attacks reminiscent of the 2008 Mumbai massacres carried out by Pakistani jihadists aligned with al-Qaeda.

When it comes to lampoon, *Charlie Hebdo* is an equal-opportunity purveyor, with no religion immune from its japery. In one religion, however, a large plurality of adherents abide neither lampoon nor *égalité* – to say nothing of *liberté*, *fraternité*, the supremacy of reason, and other pillars of Western enlightenment. It was only by mocking the tenets and excesses of that religion – Islam – that the magazine became a terrorist target.

Charbonnier was presiding over the year's first editorial meeting on the morning of Jan. 7, 2015, when Chérif and Saïd Kouachi, brandishing Kalashnikov rifles, stormed *Charlie Hebdo*'s Paris offices. Besides the journalists, they killed a maintenance worker and two unarmed police officers – one assigned as Charbonnier's bodyguard, the other a Muslim just doing his duty for France.

The brothers had at least one accomplice, Ahmedy Coulibaly, who had pledged loyalty to the infamously barbaric Islamic State, also known as ISIS or ISIL – as in the Islamic State of Iraq and al-Sham (greater Syria), or the Levant. Hours after the *Charlie Hebdo* siege, Coulibaly shot and severely wounded a jogger in a southwestern suburb of Paris. The following day, consistent with ISIS's call for Muslims to assassinate Western security personnel, Coulibaly shot and killed unarmed Paris police officer Clarissa Jean-Philippe.

Finally, he homed in on another favorite jihadist target, Jews. On Jan. 9, Coulibaly took

---

*When it comes to lampoon,* Charlie Hebdo *is an equal-opportunity purveyor, with no religion immune from its japery.*

---

hostages at a kosher supermarket in eastern Paris, warning that he would kill his captives if harm came to the Kouachis. By then, in nearby Dammartin-en-Goele, security forces surrounded the brothers, who were holding hostages in a printing factory. Ultimately, French authorities stormed both locations, shooting all three terrorists to death, but not before Coulibaly killed four of his hostages.

The eminent historian Bernard Lewis has predicted that Europe will be Islamic by the end of the 21st century, "part of the Arabic West, the Maghreb." The story of the three jihadists who terrorized France is a story of modern, transitional Europe: its open door to Muslim immigration, the antiassimilation activism of its Muslim leaders, and the jihadists who are inexorably produced.

The Kouachi brothers had been born in Paris in the early 1980s to Algerian immigrants. Orphaned, they bounced around the nearby suburbs, or *banlieues*, so many of which have become Islamic enclaves. Like an alarming number of young French Muslims, both were trained jihadists, wending their way from radical French mosques to the training camps of al-Qaeda's franchise in Yemen.

Though they roamed France freely, the brothers were known to the authorities as would-be terrorists. Chérif, in fact, had been arrested in 2005 while trying to join the anti-American jihad in Iraq. Three years later, he was briefly imprisoned for recruiting on behalf of al-Qaeda in Iraq, the franchise that eventually evolved into ISIS. It was during a prison stay that he befriended Coulibaly, another young French Muslim born to immigrants (from Mali) who was serving a bank-robbery sentence. The two men fell in with an al-Qaeda recruiter, Djamel Beghal, then serving a 10-year sentence for conspiring to bomb the American embassy in Paris. Beghal, an eminence in Europe's growing jihadist circles, had found al-Qaeda while he was a regular at London's infamous Finsbury mosque.

When the time came for their jihad, the Kouachi brothers chose their target carefully. Al-Qaeda had placed Charbonnier on a hit list published in 2013 by *Inspire*, the terrorist network's English-language magazine. Upon bursting into the editorial conference room, the brothers called him by his nom de plume – "Charb!" – before killing him in cold blood. As they fled the scene after the shooting spree, the Kouachis treated stunned survivors and spectators to the signature jihadist cries of *"Allahu Akbar!"* ("Allah is greater!") They added a chilling coda: "We have avenged the Prophet Muhammad! We have killed *Charlie Hebdo*!"

It is little wonder he was targeted. Charbonnier was a steadfast champion of free expression. His was not a hollow, hashtag courage.

In 2006, despite radical Islam's notoriously savage approach to registering disapproval, *Charlie Hebdo* republished the unflattering cartoons of Islam's prophet that were first run by Denmark's *Jyllands-Posten* newspaper. In its way, the magazine made clear that its rebuke was aimed at Islamists, not Muslims in general. The cover of the issue republish-ing the cartoons featured a weeping prophet under the headline, "*Mahomet débordé par les intégristes*" ("Muhammad overwhelmed by fundamentalists").

It is a measure of the West's decline that this served only to distinguish *Charlie Hebdo* from the major-media echo chamber. According to the latter, it was *the cartoons*, not *sharia supremacist ideology*, that "ignited" the rioting in Islamic societies across the Middle East and Central Asia. It was as if, because mayhem and murder are now the *predictable* Muslim reaction to trifling slights, they are also somehow the *rational* reaction.

Another flashing indicator of Western decline: the magazine also distinguished itself by displaying the actual cartoons. Even after the deadly rioting had patently made them a news story, such pied pipers of elite opinion as the *New York Times*, the *Washington Post*, and network news divisions on both sides of the Atlantic declined to publish them. Yale University Press even banned the cartoons from a book about – yes – *the cartoons*. And

*Jyllands-Posten* itself declined a request to republish the cartoons, with the telling admission, "Violence works."

In a schizophrenic France, *Charlie Hebdo*'s defiance left it in an ambivalent space. To be sure, official deference to free-expression principles made it the beneficiary of heightened – if ultimately ineffectual – police protection. But the republic is deracinating from its centuries-old foundation of vibrant political expression and secularist civil society. Consequently, the magazine was also subjected to no small amount of public scorn, its precarious state seen as self-induced. This is the fecklessness, the cultural self-loathing, and the soft bigotry of low expectations that induce Western opinion elites to forfeit such core liberties as free speech on the grounds that by dint of its incorrigibility, Muslim aggression has achieved entitlement status.

It is the mindset that whets radical Islam's appetite.

On Sept. 11, 2012, jihadists stormed an American diplomatic compound in Benghazi,

Libya. The terrorists murdered the United States ambassador and three other American officials. Fraudulently, but in a manner entirely consistent with the conventional wisdom that trivial insults to Islam rationalize mass murder by Muslims, the Obama administration blamed the terrorist attack (or "protest," as officials gingerly described it) on an obscure

---

*Charbonnier was a steadfast champion of free expression. His was not a hollow, hashtag courage.*

---

anti-Islamic video – a trailer for a prophet-mocking film called *Innocence of Muslims* that virtually no one on earth had actually seen.

During the eight-hour Benghazi siege, President Obama, the commander in chief of the world's only superpower, failed to take any action to defend Americans fighting for their lives. He had limitless energy, though, for mounting a lugubrious defense of Muslim rage. Obama and Hillary Clinton, his then secretary of state (and now the putative Democratic candidate to replace him), filmed public-service announcements for the consumption of Islamic audiences overseas – not to condemn the killing of Americans and the rioting at U.S. facilities in several Muslim countries, but to reassure Muslims that the American government's only involvement in *Innocence of Muslims* was to deplore its anti-Islamic themes.

And to prosecute its producer. Under the guise of a parole violation for a prior, relatively minor fraud conviction, the administration shamefully trumped up a case against Nakoula Basseley Nakoula. The film producer is an Egyptian-born Coptic Christian, then residing in California – where the First Amendment still supposedly applies, obliging government officials to *secure* our liberties, including political or artistic expression, however distasteful they may find it.

Yet in the administration's calculus, *deny-*

*ing* Nakoula's liberty was a double bonus. Domestically, with the president campaigning for re-election, jailing the producer bolstered the fraudulent narrative that the anti-Muslim video – rather than the Islamist terrorist network that Obama claimed to have "decimated" – was responsible for the Benghazi massacre. For the consumption of overseas Islamic audiences, Nakoula's plight stood as a monitory example that this American president was willing to enforce sharia blasphemy standards.

It was hardly the only such example. Just two weeks after the Benghazi massacre, Obama also used his much anticipated annual speech before the United Nations General Assembly to declare, "The future must not belong to those who slander the prophet of Islam."

At *Charlie Hebdo*, the response to Islamic supremacist aggression was markedly different. As we've seen, after Muslims rioted over the Danish cartoons, the magazine republished them. On cue, Islamists began phase one of their tried-and-true Western strategy of "First lawfare, then warfare." A Muslim activist group sued *Charlie Hebdo* under France's elastic "hate speech" laws. The magazine's retort was to mock the Islamists' mirthless intolerance. It published more cartoons, including a cover caricature of a Muslim imam, arm in arm with an equally angry-looking bishop and rabbi, demanding that *Charlie Hebdo* "be veiled." A 2011 edition featured a smiling Muhammad on the cover, promising "100 lashes if you don't die of laughter" (and, further, inviting the prophet to become the magazine's "guest editor").

By then, a French court had decided the Islamist lawsuit in favor of *Charlie Hebdo*. In the Western rule-of-law tradition, litigants are expected to accept judicial rulings against them. In radical Islam's lawfare-then-warfare tradition, when a Western court disregards sharia blasphemy standards, dissatisfied Islamists turn to phase two, the surer methods of extortion. Thus it was that in 2011, Islamists exploded a petrol bomb that destroyed *Charlie Hebdo*'s offices. And let's again be clear that it was *radical Islam*, not the cartoons, that did the igniting.

The magazine persevered, moving to a new, ostensibly more secure location and continuing to satirize Islam's excesses, just as it satirized all things political, social, and religious. As Charbonnier once put it, "We have to carry on until Islam has been rendered as banal as Catholicism."

Later in 2011, a cover depicted the prophet as a gay man kissing a male *Charlie Hebdo* cartoonist. Islamists subsequently hacked the magazine's website, but still it persisted. In so doing, *Charlie Hebdo* made plain that Muslims were not being singled out, echoing the "progressive" moral equivalence that portrays extremism as an attribute of religion in general – as if it might just as readily be Zoroastrians and Presbyterians throwing gay men to their deaths from Syrian rooftops. The magazine dutifully limned the violent jihadists not as excessively devout Muslims but as traitors to the Islam of Muhammad. In one cartoon, for instance, an ISIS terrorist was depicted beheading the prophet after condemning him as an "infidel."

The nuances did not impress the intended audience. The week after the Sept. 11, 2012, wave of anti-American attacks, *Charlie Hebdo* lampooned the Obama administration's risible

---

*It is a measure of the West's decline that this served only to distinguish* Charlie Hebdo *from the major-media echo chamber.*

---

suggestion that a video, however provocative, could rationalize murder, maiming, and property destruction. It ran caricatures of a naked Muhammad in the pages of an edition whose cover cartoon displayed the prophet in a wheelchair pushed by an Orthodox Jew under the headline *"Intouchables."*

The issue was published over the objections of the French government – the same

[ 14 ]

government that would later take center stage at the postmassacre *Je Suis Charlie* rally. The Obama administration also complained. With the president taking election-season heat over his implication that civilized people could be incited to commit the Benghazi atrocities by a harmless video, White House spokesman Jay Carney grudgingly conceded that Obama was not claiming *Charlie Hebdo*'s publication "justified" violence, but the administration nonetheless faulted the magazine's "judgment" in choosing to exercise its "right" to free expression.

Obama, meanwhile, used his own judgment to rail about "slanders" against "the prophet of Islam" from his U.N. soapbox ... while al-Qaeda used its judgment to put Charbonnier on a hit list. The rest is history.

Yet how did we get to this historical anomaly in which, as the estimable scholar Daniel Pipes observes, "a majority population accepts the customs and even the criminality of a poorer and weaker immigrant community"? It is the result of a conquest ideology taking the measure of a civilization that no longer values its heritage, no longer regards itself as worthy of defense.

France's population of 66 million is now approximately 10 percent Islamic. Estimates are sketchy because, in a vestige of its vanishing secularist tradition, France does not collect census data about religious affiliation. Still, between 6 million and 7 million Muslims are reasonably believed to reside in the country. (Pew put the total at 4.7 million back in 2010; other analysts peg it higher today.) To many in France, the number seems higher, because of both the outsize influence of Islamist activists on the political class and the dense Muslim communities in and around Paris – approximating 15 percent of the local population. An online poll conducted by Ipsos MORI in 2014 found that the average French citizen *believes* Muslims make up about a third of the country's population.

As night follows day, when Muslim populations surge, so does support for jihadism and the sharia supremacist ideology that catalyzes it. The reason is plain to see, even if Western elites remain willfully blind to it. For a not-insignificant percentage of the growing Muslim millions in Europe, infiltration – by both mass immigration and the establishment of swelling Islamic enclaves – is a purposeful strategy of conquest, sometimes referred to as "voluntary apartheid."

One of its leading advocates is Sheikh Yusuf al-Qaradawi. A Qatar-based Egyptian octogenarian, al-Qaradawi is a Muslim Brotherhood icon. He is a copiously published scholar who graduated from Cairo's al-Azhar University, the seat of Sunni Islamic learning for over a millennium, and thus oversees both the International Union of Muslim Scholars and the European Council for Fatwa and Research. Thanks to his pioneering of the highly trafficked IslamOnline website and, especially, to his hugely popular al-Jazeera television program *Sharia and Life*, he has become the world's most influential sharia jurist.

Al-Qaradawi is the sharia backbone of the

violent jihad to exterminate Israel — a tiny country surrounded by hundreds of millions of hostile Muslims. The sheikh also vows that Islam will "conquer" both Europe and America but acknowledges that this conquest will require a strategy more suited to a determined minority that knows it cannot win by force of arms alone. The key, he asserts, is *dawa*, the Muslim equivalent of proselytism. In radical Islam, it is hyperaggressive, pushing on every cultural cylinder, pressuring every institution, and exploiting the atmosphere of intimidation created by jihadist terrorism to blur the lines between legal advocacy and extortion.

In France, *dawa* presses against *laïcité*, the credo of secularism through the strict separation of religion and the state. Al-Qaradawi is quite clear that "secularism can never enjoy a general acceptance in an Islamic society." He is equally adamant that Muslims, who are bound to live in accordance with the strictures of sharia, must reject a secular framework because "acceptance of secularism means abandonment of sharia, a denial of the divine guidance and a rejection of Allah's injunctions." Thus, he elaborates, "the call for secularism among Muslims is atheism and a rejection of Islam. Its acceptance as a basis for rule in place of sharia is downright apostasy."

This nexus between free speech and Western democracy is worth pausing over. Notice that in focusing on the incompatibility between Islamic law and democracy's secular, pluralist underpinnings, al-Qaradawi draws the inevitable conclusion that democracy equals apostasy. The term *apostasy* is not invoked idly in Islam. As explained in *Reliance of the Traveller*, a classic sharia manual endorsed by al-Azhar scholars, the renunciation of Islam is a death-penalty offense.

Free speech does not exist in a vacuum. It is the plinth of freedom's fortress. It is the ineliminable imperative if there is to be the robust exchange of knowledge and ideas, the rule of reason, freedom of conscience, equality before the law, property rights, and equality of opportunity. That is why it must be extin-

*France is deracinating from the principles of vibrant political expression and secularist civil society, its foundation for centuries.*

guished if there is to be what al-Qaradawi calls a "place of religion" – meaning *his* religion. For all its arrogance and triumphalist claims, radical Islam must suppress speech because it cannot compete in a free market of conscience.

To sustain their movement, therefore, Islamist leaders must separate Muslims from secular society. In the West, this means forming Islamic enclaves in which sharia gradually takes root as the de facto and, eventually, the de jure law – enabling Muslims to resist the challenge of critical thinking under the guise of avoiding the near occasion of apostasy. Over time, dominion is established over swaths of not only physical territory but also legal privilege. Al-Qaradawi puts the matter succinctly:

> *Were we to convince Western leaders and decision-makers of our right to live according to our faith – ideologically, legislatively, and ethically – without imposing our views or inflicting harm upon them, we would have traversed an immense barrier in our quest for an Islamic state.*

The key to the conquest strategy is to coerce the West into accepting a Muslim right to resist assimilation, to regard sharia as superseding Western law and custom when the two conflict. For precisely this reason, the Organization of Islamic Cooperation – a bloc of 56 Muslim countries (plus the Palestinian Authority) – has decreed that "Muslims should not be marginalized or attempted to be assimilated, but should be accommodated." Recep Tayyip Erdogan, the Islamist president of Turkey who has systematically dismantled that country's secular, pro-Western system, similarly pronounces that pressuring Muslims to assimilate in the West "is a crime against humanity."

Free expression is the gateway to assimilation. Consequently, radical Islam cannot tolerate it.

As a result, France is now rife with *zones urbaines sensibles* – "sensitive urban areas." The government officially lists some 751 of them: Islamic enclaves in the *banlieues,* often referred to as no-go zones because the indigenous populations discourage the presence of non-Muslims who do not conform to Islamic standards of dress and social interaction, and of public officials – police, firefighters, emergency medical teams, and building inspectors – who are seen as symbols of the state's effort to exercise sovereignty in areas that Muslims seek to possess adversely.

Some of those zones inevitably evolve into hotbeds of jihadist activity. As the Gatestone Institute's Soeren Kern notes, citing a report by the Middle East Media Research Institute, there has been no shortage of Internet traffic suggesting, for example, "the killing of France's ambassadors, just as the 'manly' Libyan fighters killed the U.S. ambassador in Benghazi." In a low-intensity jihadist thrum stretching back several years, the torching of automobiles has become commonplace: as many as 40,000 cars are burned annually. Perhaps most alarmingly, over a thousand French Muslims, more than from any other Western country, are estimated to have traveled to Syria to fight for ISIS – meaning many will return to the country as trained, battle-hardened jihadists. Beyond the direct ISIS participants, moreover, the *Washington Post* has reported that a recent poll found 16 percent of French citizens expressing some degree of support for ISIS – an organization whose rule over the vast territory it has seized is best known for decapitations, rapine, burning prisoners alive, the execution of homosexuals, mass graves, and the enslavement of non-Muslim communities.

Once one grasps the voluntary-apartheid strategy, it becomes obvious why radical

Islam's inroads in France, and elsewhere in Europe, seamlessly translate into demands for the enforcement of sharia's curbs on speech and artistic expression. What is not so obvious is just what a profound challenge to the West this constitutes.

The shocking *Charlie Hebdo* atrocity called global attention to the offensive caricatures, as well as renewed attention to the Danish cartoons, the *Innocence of Muslims* trailer, and other instances in which Islam's detractors have resorted to insult – what Obama breezily distorts as "slander" – to make their points. The focus on blatant provocation grievously minimizes the stakes of the Islamist threat.

Even free-speech enthusiasts are repulsed by obnoxious expression. One who passionately argues that it would be perilously wrong to *criminalize*, say, flag burning or the exhibition of Andres Serrano's *Piss Christ* can sympathize with calls to *discourage* their display – privately, nonthreateningly, and within the bounds of the law. After all, few sensible people would miss expression that is in poor taste and edifies neither our political discourse nor our appreciation of beauty. From that seemingly benign premise, however, it is but a short leap to the dangerous conclusion that *an outright ban* on sheer insults to Islam would be a harmless accommodation: "Yes, it would betray free-expression principles, but," we soothe ourselves, "it might serve the worthy cause of social harmony."

---

*When Muslim populations surge, so does support for jihadism and the sharia supremacist ideology that catalyzes it.*

---

In fact, it would do exactly the opposite. A conquest ideology takes well-meaning accommodation as weakness and always demands more. But that is almost beside the point, because what is at risk is so much more than the right to give gratuitous offense.

As the aforementioned sharia manual *Reliance of the Traveller* instructs, classical Islamic law's suppression of artistic expression is not limited to mere sacrilege. It forbids depictions of "animate life," which are deemed offensive to Allah because they "imitate [his] creative act." "Whoever makes a picture," the manual warns, "Allah shall torture him with it on the Day of Judgment." So put aside the palpable fact that insult is frequently provocative in an enlightening, socially productive way. What is ultimately at stake in radical Islam's challenge to the West is art itself – in all its bracing genius and poignant presentation.

Perhaps even more ominous is the challenge to political speech outside the realm of art. Sharia's death penalty for apostasy is well known. What is not well known, however, is the breadth of conduct that sharia regards as apostasy. It is not limited to a Muslim's renunciation of Islam. There are various forms of what we might call "constructive apostasy" – for example, idol worship, the utterance of "words that imply unbelief," statements that appear to deny or revile Allah or the Prophet Muhammad, denial of "the obligatory character" of something scholarly consensus makes part of Islam, and even mere sarcasm regarding "any ruling of the Sacred Law." The enormity of prohibited expression far transcends *Charlie Hebdo*–style effrontery.

Hand in hand with apostasy, Islam prohibits blasphemy – by both Muslims and non-Muslims. "Wait," you're thinking, "how can a religion make rules for nonbelievers?" But remember: Islam, particularly in its extremist construction, perceives itself as not simply a religion but a full-blown societal framework, one that abides no division between private belief and public governance. It dictates terms to nonbelievers because it aims to rule them, at Allah's direction and under Allah's law.

Sharia is quite intentionally less indulgent of non-Muslims. Islamists and their apologists never tire of telling credulous Westerners that Islam permits no compulsion in matters of religion. This, however, merely means non-

> *Free speech does not exist in a vacuum. It is the plinth of freedom's fortress.*

Muslims are not forced to *convert*. By contrast, Islam *does compel the imposition of sharia*. That is where compulsion comes in, for non-Muslims as well as Muslims. The system is designed to encourage conversion without forcing conversation, by making it starkly more attractive to be a Muslim. Sharia thus pervasively discriminates against non-Muslims (*dhimmis*): relegating them to lower-caste status, coercing their payment of a poll tax (*jizya*) for the privilege of living as infidels in an Islamic state, and exhorting Muslims to make them feel humiliated. In this, Muslim law fulfills Allah's command in the Koran's Sura 9:29:

*Fight those who believe not in Allah nor the Last Day, nor hold forbidden which had been forbidden by Allah and his Messenger, nor acknowl-*

*edge the Religion of Truth, from among the people of the book* [i.e., Christians and Jews], *until they pay the* jizya *and feel themselves subdued.*

As should be apparent, the radical Islamic interpretation of sharia is even less tolerant of perceived slights to Islam by nonbelievers than it is of irreverent displays – constructive apostasy – by Muslims. To constitute blasphemy, speech need not be insulting or slanderous. Islamists deem critical examinations of Islam to be blasphemous, especially if they reach negative conclusions or encourage unbelief. Proselytism of religions other than Islam, particularly if it involves encouraging Muslims to abandon Islam, is also strictly forbidden. In sum, if speech or expression could sow discord among Muslims or within an Islamic community, sharia would prohibit it. And truth is not a defense.

Clearly, the encroachment of sharia and its blasphemy standards in the West is not about whether a satirist should be permitted to caricature Muhammad as a gay man or salaciously discuss the aging prophet's scripturally documented connubial relations with a 9-year-old girl. It is about whether a society targeted by radical Islam can be prevented from understanding the threat and can defend itself. It is about whether a free society retains the wherewithal to engage in robust political discourse, the sine qua non of self-government.

That is the challenge. So what is the response?

France is at the forefront of the transnational progressive march toward a postnational, politically homogenous Europe that dances to the tune called by technocrats in Brussels. Classical Western liberalism is strictly déclassé.

French leaders have enmeshed the country in such multilateral treaties as the European Convention on Human Rights, the International Convention on the Elimination of All Forms of Racial Discrimination, and the International Covenant on Civil and Political Rights. As the Middle East Forum's Lawfare

Project details, this burgeoning corpus of international law pays lip service to freedom of expression but sedulously restricts it with ever more elastic protections "of the reputation and rights of others." The treaties direct member states to enact nebulous laws that render illegal "the dissemination of ideas based on racial superiority or hatred," as well as "advocacy" of "religious hatred" that could be an "incitement to ... hostility."

French law, too, bans "hate speech," defined to include incitement to racial discrimination or "hatred" based on, inter alia, one's religious group. In effect, this hopelessly politicized pandering has empowered the Muslim grievance industry to criminalize aspersions against Islam. To heighten the *in terrorem* effect on the masses, legal action has been taken against prominent citizens. Legendary actress Brigitte Bardot has been convicted and fined several times – most recently for speaking against the ritual slaughter of sheep during a Muslim feast. Controversial politician Jean-Marie Le Pen (runner-up in the 2002 presidential election) was convicted for bewailing the anti-assimilationist consequences of Muslim immigration. And though ultimately acquitted (by a court that sidestepped the "incitement" issue), author Michel Houellebecq endured protracted legal proceedings after he publicly described Islam as "stupid" and "dangerous."

Of course, France has no First Amendment. Notwithstanding its enlightened tradition, it has always been easier to ban varieties of expression there than in the United States. In fact, in an overreaction to the crisis of internal strife largely self-induced by its sundry accommodations of radical Islam, France has banned Muslim women from donning the burka (the fully enveloping garment that covers even the face) in public places. The ban is probably counterproductive: its non-enforcement in Islamic enclaves only promotes the conceit that sharia has superseded French law. But unwise or not, the First Amendment would not tolerate such a ban.

Nevertheless, if President Obama has his

> *A conquest ideology takes well-meaning accommodation as weakness and always demands more.*

way, the First Amendment will yield to sharia blasphemy standards. In conjunction with the aforementioned Organization of Islamic Cooperation (OIC), Obama's then Secretary of State Clinton sponsored United Nations Human Rights Council Resolution 16/18. It calls on all governments to outlaw "any advocacy of religious hatred against individuals that constitutes incitement to discrimination, hostility or violence." In arrant violation of the Constitution, the resolution would accomplish what Obama has sought since his first days in office: speech suppression predicated on mob intimidation.

In parsing the provision, bear in mind that incitement to violence is already criminalized throughout the United States, and discrimination based on race, sex, age, ethnicity, religion, and sexual preference is outlawed by numerous federal and state laws and regulations. Resolution 16/18 has only one purpose: to render illegal speech that could cause Muslims to perceive hostility toward their belief system – under circumstances in which even those who hold Islam in disfavor are not trying to ban it, and where mere hostility (a) may not be prohibited under our law, (b) is a prudent and natural response to many provocations, and (c) ironically is to be subjected to an unprecedented ban for the benefit of Islam, the scriptures and laws of which are inherently hostile to non-Muslims, women, and homosexuals.

The resolution so starkly transgresses the First Amendment that its chief proponent, Hillary Clinton, had to be armed with a plan B – something even more breathtakingly repressive. At a meeting of the "Istanbul Process" she had confederated with OIC leaders, after the customary lip-service tribute to free expression (a "universal right at the core of our democracy"), she vowed that the Obama administration would "use some old-fashioned techniques of peer pressure and shaming, so that people don't feel that they have the support to do what we abhor." Translation: government-supported extortion tactics, the Constitution be damned.

Thus does sharia suppression of speech become just one more weapon in the left's indoctrination arsenal. It is a ceaseless jihad to convert our politics, the campus, the media, and the broader culture into "progressive" enclaves. In these no-go zones, nonconforming expression, dissent, and individual liberty are suffocated by speech codes (informal or, increasingly, codified), campaigns for social and academic "justice" (where the search for excellence and truth are subordinated to left-wing mythology and piety), the push for "net neutrality" (to strangle by regulation the conservative and libertarian voices that have thrived in the Internet's free market), economic boycotts (to cripple the corporate sponsorship of competing ideas), and campaign finance reform (to suppress political speech under the guise of anticorruption). The principal target is "hatred," a strategically vague term that can be invoked to ban anything the left opposes.

Shortly after the *"Je Suis Charlie"* signs and the sunshine patriots melted away, *Le Journal du Dimanche*, a weekly newspaper, released some poll results. Less than two weeks had elapsed since the slaughter and the lionizing of gadfly cartoonists as free-speech martyrs, yet 42 percent of French citizens opposed the

---

*France is at the forefront of the transnational progressive march toward a postnational, politically homogenous Europe that dances to the tune called by technocrats in Brussels.*

---

publication of *Charlie Hebdo*'s cartoons. Echoing the political class, they agreed that action should be taken to avoid giving offense to Muslims.

By early February, a thousand protesters who were assembled by the Muslim Action Forum demonstrated outside the British Ministry of Defence in London. Under a sign warning Britons to "Be Careful With Muhammad," the leaders distributed leaflets that condemned the use of "freedom of speech" to "sow the seeds of hatred" and "damage community relations" by "provoking Muslims." The British government, whose leaders had joined the *Je Suis Charlie* rally just a month earlier, responded by . . . investigating citizens who purchased issues of *Charlie Hebdo* – in the interest of "enhancing public safety" and "assessing community tensions," of course.

Like the Obama administration, they know they are not Charlie. What they may not know is that their security depends on giving offense to radical Islam, the breed of Muslim that aims to conquer them.

First American edition published in 2015 by Encounter Books, an activity of Encounter for Culture and Education, Inc., a nonprofit, tax exempt corporation. Encounter Books website address: www.encounterbooks.com

Manufactured in the United States and printed on acid-free paper. The paper used in this publication meets the minimum requirements of ANSI/NISO Z39.48–1992 (R 1997) (*Permanence of Paper*).

FIRST AMERICAN EDITION

LIBRARY OF CONGRESS CATALOGING-IN-PUBLICATION DATA

McCarthy, Andrew C.
Islam and free speech / by Andrew C. McCarthy.
pages    cm
ISBN 978-1-59403-748-1 (pbk. : alk. paper) —
ISBN 978-1-59403-749-8 (ebook)
1. Freedom of speech—Religious aspects—Islam.  I. Title.
BL173.66M33 2015
323.44'3—dc23
2015007204

10 9 8 7 6 5 4 3 2 1

SERIES DESIGN BY CARL W. SCARBROUGH